Things No One Else Wants to Say

By

Micah the Poet

Published by Capturing Fire Press, Washington, DC

ISBN: 978-1-7328759-4-4

Capturing Fire Press is an independent publishing house founded by Regie Cabico that seeks to promote politically charged, performance & experimental poetry of the highest quality by diverse queer poets from around the globe.

Copyright 2020 by Capturing Fire Press

All rights reserved. No part of this book may be reproduced, scanned, or distributed in any printed or electronic form without permission of the publisher or the author. All inquired and permissions requests should be addressed to the author at:
micahthepoet@gmail.com.

Cover art by
Rich Rocket | iamrichrocket.co/rich-rocket-media

Manuscript and book cover layout by
Sasha Sinclair | Studio 3440 | studio3440.com

Printed in the United States of America

- INTRODUCTION 3
- **FAMILY** 5
  - WORDS FOR MY FATHER 8
  - DADDY'S GIRL 10
  - CONVOS WITH MY BROTHER 12
  - LETTERS BETWEEN BLACK MEN (PART 1) 13
  - LETTERS BETWEEN BLACK MEN (PART 2) 14
  - HIS EULOGY 15
  - FOR BLAKE 16
  - STORY FROM JILL 18
  - BEARD GANG 20
  - FOR HOPE 21
  - FOR THE GIRLS OF CHIBOK: 23
  - THE FUTURE 25
- **LIFE** 27
  - ROOTS 29
  - THE JAR 30
  - SONGS 32
  - THOUGHTS OF MAYA 34
  - EAR TO THE STREETS 35
  - ODE TO PLAY, PLAY POETS 37
  - LONELY 38
  - NOTE ON LIFE #1 39
  - NOVOCAIN 40
  - LIFETIMES: A SHORT STORY 41
  - STUPID QUESTIONS 43
  - ODE TO THE LORDS OF THE STREET: 44
  - NOTE ON LIFE #2 45
  - THAT ONE TIME I WAS GONNA RAP 46
  - ME AND MY MANS JAY 47
  - B-L-A-C-K 48

NOTE ON LIFE #3	50
BLACK GIRL MAGIC	51
HANDS UP	52
TROUBLES OF TIME	54
PANDORA'S BOX	56
NOTE ON LIFE #4	58
LETTER FROM A QUEER TO THE WORLD	59
LETTER TO THE BIGOT	61
NOTE ON LIFE #5	62
SACRIFICE IS SO SACRILEGE	63
NOTES ON LIFE #6	65
NOTE ON LIFE #7	67

LOVE 69

LOVE THEORY	71
REAL LOVE: THE DEFINITION	72
UNIVERSAL LANGUAGE	74
MAKING IT THROUGH 2:36 AM	76
BOOGIE MAN	77
GETTING LATE	80
DAYDREAMS IN ANAPHORA	82
DAY AT THE BEACH	83
HOW'S THE WEATHER	84
NOTE ON LIFE #8	85
PRETTY LITTLE THINGS	86
IF I COULD SING	87
HOW TO EXPLAIN THE WAY YOU WANT TO BE LOVED TO THE PERSON THAT YOU LOVE	89
I KEPT	90
DIRTY, DIRTY LOVE	91
BLESS-ED BE	93
THE PROTOTYPE	95
TIMES	97
LIVING VS SURVIVING	98

PLEASE DON'T GO, WE'LL EAT YOU UP..........100
WE LOVE YOU SO!..100
WALK WITH ME..102
RED BLACK AND GREEN QUEEN......................104

For Martheia, Ivory, Geneva, and Rob.
My first audience.

INTRODUCTION

rabble-rouser: rab·ble-rous·er

/ˈrabəl ˌrouzər/: a person who speaks with the intention of inflaming the emotions of a crowd of people...

My brother used to say I have a way with words- a manner of speaking that would always make one listen, or at the very least feel. When I was young, I told him I would write a book. He said, "You should name it, *Things No one Else Wants to Say*. That's what you do, you say what we're all feeling and take the heat so we can learn and be better." I never thought anyone was watching that close. My Mama kept me away from crowds, large schools, and protests. I wasn't allowed to excite people with my words at first, but I had a knack for telling the truth and speaking plainly about things in a way people could relate to. It didn't take long for her to give in and let me start performing.

In my experience, the truth does two things; it makes us see and it hurts a little. Both are embarrassing, but neither of those things ever really bothered me much. I just have never felt like I had any reason to be ashamed. We all make mistakes. We all make poor choices, we all live in sin, and we all have dark secrets. What makes me feel better is knowing, really knowing, that it's OK. It's ok to let it out, it's ok to talk about it, it's ok to feel. There is a space for all of us in this world, and I think that's what I wanted to express when I wrote this. I wanted to write something that people could relate to, find words for things they were feeling, or to express to a loved one. These writings are from the last 20 YEARS of my human experience. Some I wrote a year ago, some I wrote when I was 11. This book is a more of a memoir than a collection of poems. There are some short stories in here, some journal entries, some raps, some poetry; little bit of everything. It's split into three parts: Love, Life, and Family. These are ideals that I feel have shaped who I am today. They are three aspects of the human experience that are cyclical and feed off one another. I grow, experience, mature, and evolve with every breath I take. We all do. Hopefully, within the pages of this book, you'll find a voice, a smile, understanding, empowerment, or maybe just some silent solidarity. I love y'all. Thank you for taking the time to read some of my work.

-Micah the Poet

FAMILY

Family is very intersectional for me. I belong to many families outside of my blood lineage. Outside of them, I have my African American family, my poetry family, my queer family, and various other families that I've formed over the years. Family for me is a connectedness I share with people in addition to my actual blood family. All my families have always been uplifting and supportive of my life. Although, thinking back now. I think that is in large part due to having a very protective mother and grandmother that did not play about my safety, security, and well-being.

I did experience divorce on some level. I wasn't home much, but my father left the immediate family when I was around 14. I was told it was a big thing and my father made some very poor choices, but I was going to school, performing, travelling etc. the concept of a biological present father figure was forlorn, but I had other father figures, so I was ok. My father was out of sight out of mind most days, and the days that he was on my mind, I wrote about it. I think I just always felt bad because everyone always said he was missing out on so much. We've been cordial over the years. I guess after I grew up there wasn't much to say in real life, and I don't really know him well.

There are things that I wish he could hear, but I just put them in this book.

My Mama is the most important person in my life. Period. She's quite holy to me. Everything good I've learned in life has pretty much came from her. (including my life) My brother is my rock. There is no one in this world that understands me like he does.

In this chapter there are poems about families that I have felt connected to, people that I feel are my brothers, sisters, aunties, uncles, mothers, fathers etc. Some poems are about my biological family, some poems are about self-made families. This chapter is the shortest. What can I say? I am blessed to have been grown in nutrient rich soil, the good, bad, and indifferent shaped this brown child beautifully.

WORDS FOR MY FATHER

These are the words I wish my Father could hear, you know, if he was right here
I'm standing tall
I've defended myself against being mauled, bound, gagged, and assaulted
I even fought the walls like Luke Skywalker
Remember?
I told you I would

These days I try and walk the line
I had a breaking point just like you
Still trying to find a love that I can trust and devote myself to
Remember?
You said there's no life without devotion

You were like my schoolbooks
I wanted to talk, walk, act like you
Like I was Mogli and you were Baloo
Now all I have is a broken heart where Scars have killed my Mufasa in you
It's because of us I learned the meaning behind the blues
I learned to put melancholy in my poetry

I went away to college to hone my art
Instead of dealing with the mess we made of we
It was easier to speak to strangers on dark stages and sing of dreams than to face reality
Waking up still drunk face down on vomit-soaked linoleum floors on the nights after I tried to forget you
Long morning pees signaling the end of unicorns and making believe I never met you

I expected you to leave when you could no longer look at me

Around 12-13
When you began distancing yourself to lessen the pain of me losing my main man

While my heart is still broken from Mama's tear-filled Dear John pen strokes
My heart still evokes passion for a man with demons

Daddy?
Oh, it's been about ten years since I've seen him

But if you're ever watching a show on poets and they show this performance
I want you to know I forgive you and I love you
Or maybe I just think I do because I have to
Really, there's just no other way to get past you
No need to worry dad, I've done exactly what you told me to
Remember?
You said,
"Do what I say baby, never as I do"

DADDY'S GIRL

You can't keep a daughter from her daddy
I mean
Even if you take her daddy
She still fiend for that man love
Get them body shots and call him daddy
Daddy
She is yearning, moaning because she miss her daddy

She went from
Waiting for him at the window
To
Waiting for him at the window

She miss her daddy

She's clinging to his remainder
The space he left is her pacifier
And aren't we all nostalgic

When a daughter's first heartbreak comes from her father
Every man after becomes a martyr to the religion she has found
In worshiping his absence

She becomes a bad girl that does bad things
Cause Daddy's not watching
And mama just can't hurt the same
Even if mama leaves

Daddy used to promise her and sing

"If that mockingbird don't sing, daddy's gonna buy you a diamond ring"
So, she waits for her daddy, because the mockingbird quit mocking her a long time ago

Now

She holds echoes
Shadows of the men she made promise and sing,
"If that mockingbird don't sing, Daddy's gonna buy you a diamond ring"

CONVOS WITH MY BROTHER

Question #1: What the best thing you can make?
    BACON

Question #2: What are two things that always come back?
    Boomerangs and Pussies

LETTERS BETWEEN BLACK MEN (Part 1)

Dear black man before me,
I stand tall and proud, somehow. I'm just trying to be a black man here. Beware of me, you should be scared of me. After all they say that bad things are black things and I'm George Thorogood bad to the bone because the good define the weak and the weak don't define a black man. Not black masculinity. I'm just trying to be black man here, so what if I get ghost. Hey, some of us have daddies and some us don't. I was a black boy 15 going on 50, I ain't have time for fear. So, call me selfish or egotistical for having my own goals in view despite all of you. Even Jesus left his mother to follow his true father, but when you're a real black man you're thinking of love often. My daddy's daddy, he didn't know what dreams was, so excuse me for my infatuation with my situation in front of me, they consider me the lowest thing. The only human to ever be 3/5ths of a being. See black man before me, NOW black men must pass down the knowledge in seeing, the knowledge in dreaming. We just trying to be black men here. Damn! Can't you hear? We are human just like you, working every day, just like you, trying to make the world beautiful. In someone's eyes... but after how are we've fought we're no better than the plague. Praised in history books but never on the street, if you see a black man in jail it can't be for peace! Something about this dark skin makes you see my heart in shades of grey. Never think my actions are good for the moment, Jekyll and Hyde persona, as men naturally we do what we want to, don't mean to cause pain in the process, we did what we thought was best. But please, don't type cast me as the black guy because they always die. Just call me the black man, because black men turn into old black men, and even then, I'll still get an old lady wink, or a stare. So damn, just let me be a black man here!

Best Regards,
Your Son

LETTERS BETWEEN BLACK MEN (Part 2)

Dear Son,
400 plus years ago this overseer took away my dad and made him a boy. Just. Like. Me. How you gonna respect a man that ain't no stronger than you? So, me and my former father worked side by side like brothers, and our mother, she cared for us, our sisters, healed us, our aunties, they held our spirit until we were strong enough to tame it. I was told my father's father would have been a king. He walked erect with a nation's pride until he saw his father die. Then they put him on a boat and beat that pride from his eyes and made him forget that he was a prince, which in turn made him forget to teach me that I was better than all this. I watched him dwindle to footprints, stepping on the ground as if it owned him now. My father gave me water paints and propositioned me to portray his failures. Now I, match those prints with my feet. My father forgot that he could use his brain and forgot to pass me down mine, so all I could think was to get a better life, by any means. I didn't want to replay his scene, so I did some very strange things for change because I heard that money gives you power and we all know that change turns into dollars. I wanted to be better than that white man that took away my father. I was too dumb to see that I was a rat in a maze, to selfish trying to get that cheese I didn't bother to help you through. Now look at you, you're just diluted shades of brown trained to frown on things that LOOK different. Taught that this able black body was hardly anything but a sign that the world may weigh you down as they please, but son please, don't think of yourself a disease because the only release from that is death. Wish more for yourself.

The world is yours and you're running from it, don't play who done it, make the best of every moment. You're just trying to be a black man there, or so I hear.
Love,
Dad

HIS EULOGY

This is what my kids will probably say at my funeral.

My Papo had bright eyes and dark secrets. He had a place in his heart for everyone he met, even demons. He would tell us animated stories that guided us to where the wild things were, then quietly walk downstairs to smoke out the window. I often sat awake listening to his silent lament, his weary aching and creaking through the house, echoing through the peaceful halls of our home. My Papo would cry while he sang songs. Sway back and forth to the riffs and melodies; something about life exhaustedly thrilled him and he had found it in the voice of the music. He would build fires, even when it was warm, just so we would understand there must always be fervor. He spoke meaningfully. Or never spoke at all. Only around certain people would he flash that winning smile with the gap that gave it personality. When he was comfortable, he was a charismatic Charlie. He never waived his stance on things out of circumstance. Something's, as he would say, should just be. He could convince you of everything he could never convince himself of. He probably could have been a preacher, but they say he cussed too much. My Papo was deep as the ocean but could make things seem as simple as a puddle. I'm really gonna miss him.

He always said "Keep it simple." So, with that I'll leave it there. Simple in its own way

FOR BLAKE

"I'm sorry this world was cruel to you."
That's what the paper said. They gathered the remains of his body and had to tell his mother(s) that her child had not only decided that he had not been placed in the right body, but he had also not been placed in the right realm. This is a world that is only appealing in different shades and stages.

Dear Blake

I'M SORRY

I'm sorry you were stuck in a costume, a black faced minstrel

I'm sorry that the word "normal" bamboozled you out of your happiness

I'm sorry you had to be better than great to be relevant

I'm sorry that you just couldn't play your drums in the band with the rest of the geeks

Or just, wear baggy clothes try to claim lesbian to fill that void

I'm sorry that the life you had to look forward to
Was a life of risking life and limb just to LOOK at yourself and not feel like a clown in regular shoes

I'm sorry they called you transman, instead of just a man

Like you were somehow inferior

I'm sorry that the world in this light threw shade on you

I'm sorry for every lesbian you tried to date that said you were too much of a man

And every straight girl who said you still had girl parts

I'm sorry no one ever told you a man is measured by his faith

I'm sorry that you always had to be happy, but never felt it

I'm sorry that sometimes wholeness is found in knowing yourself and being able to express it

I'm sorry the earth just wouldn't turn and let the light shine through

Make a rainbow for you

Maybe then you would have seen,
That beauty
Is the result of rainstorms

STORY FROM JILL
(THE MASCULINE LESBIAN)
(This is poem contains real quotes from Jill)

I was walking along innocently, being me, when this girl
comes up and says, "You think you're a boy, don't you?"
I laughed hard as I responded, "Just as much as you think
you're a bitch"

I continued spouting to her stunned face
"I mean if we're just making assumptions here
Then it would be very clear that if my clothes don't fit my
ass dudes don't holler when I pass then
I must be a boy
but the fact that yours do only makes you a hoe

Oh, that's what I love about these generalizations
They can confuse a nation into a fearing a man wearing a
turban
Make politicians label everything represented by dark skin
"urban"
Make the government believe that the lower class is
undeserving

Like, every Jamaican likes to work
Asians love math and hate girls
Every American is racist
No man can turn down sex
They say, it's generally true

I'm beginning to get de'ja vu
When things were separate but equal
But even after they integrated us
We still sat with the black people
Because stereotypically we're supposed to be all about
unity
But only for my people and me

See young lady, hypocrisy breeds best in jealousy

So automatically I would have to be something less in
your eyes for you to start generalizing
Lastly, you are feeding into a label
Typed in stereo for the world to see
It's a vision of what the world expects you to be
Don't you think we should shake it up and use empathy?

Even if you don't
Do me a favor and be better Queen
Drop the assumptions next time you see me"

BEARD GANG

I told my mama *clears throat*
 I TOLD HER. I was GOING to grow a beard

She said DON'T you dare you can't, you won't. Ruin...
The strait-laced person I am making of you

I walked away from that. I AM A MAN
I'm gon do what I'm gon do

I TOLD THEM

I am GOING to grow a beard

And they said
What?? you're so young, so beautiful don't be so rash

I don't care what you think got-dammnit I'm STILL gonna look GOODT

I AM A MAN I can pull off anything

I told MY GIRLFRIEND, BABY! It's beard time

She said, Oh no! I like your soft face it's the only link I have to feminine energy with you
You are SUCH a man

I moved on from her too
Because sometimes
If they don't love the beard, they're trying to hold you back
I GREW MY BEARD

Some stayed and some didn't, some grew to love The Fuzz No matter what pretty they see now, it's mine
I made you see beauty, in a beard on me

FOR HOPE

Preface:
I love you Hope. Our memories will always replay in the back of mind. Everything has its own season and time. This was yours, but I can't wait to see you again and tell you of mine. My sister, my smile, my best friend. The reason why a soulful voice (Whatever) first escaped my lips. You will be honored for your contribution to this earth the, lives you touched will forever feel your unconditional love for life and all of the above so today.... Everyday. I say this for Hope. I am thankful for the experience of having her in my world.

Psalm 119:74:
"May those who fear you rejoice when they see me, for I have put my HOPE in your world."

See, there's proof that God sent you to bless us all.
This one's for Hope
This is for you my friend
When God sat down and formed your life, He branded you with the name of what you'd mean to everyone you ever ran across.
Hope.

People never understood why you were never cross, even though your life wasn't perfect you were never lost, you always knew God had paid the cost. So, all you had to do was make sure it wasn't in vain. My friend knew pain. Knew what it was like to feel as though she would never be whole again, but she made the best of every moment. Took life by the neck and owned it. If she was ever afraid, she never showed it. Hope always had herself. Always ready to take on the next obstacle, she had this life licked like a Popsicle. God knew he needed his angel to come home. I bet heaven just wasn't the same without her spirit, and though I had to respect it because my friend was needed. Hope taught me how to love, how to care, how to really mean it to a friend when you say you'll always be there. Hope said not to shed tears if she ever

wasn't here so, I'll just think of all we did. All SHE did. And remember to rejoice.
God didn't give us HOPE for no reason.

FOR THE GIRLS OF CHIBOK: #BRINGBACKOURGIRLS

On April 16th, 2015 I sat on my phone with my mama, talking about groceries, taking our pointless stories for granted

I know there is a woman in Chibok that can't eat because she is wondering if her daughter is eating, if she is alive

They have still not brought our girls back and no gala, fancy song, or hashtag has changed that

276 mothers woke up panicked
In a frenzy
Making their way to a future memorial site

276 mothers have been crying for 365 days
Until reality doesn't make sense

They have been through the five stages for grief every day, 73 times over

There's no closure when the books their daughters were studying aren't even closed

There's no cure for the disease of grief
How do you get by missing a piece of your heart?

One mother said,
"Some days I wake up and I just don't want to move, I don't want to breathe, I just want to be where she is"
Like if she squeezes her eyes tight enough
She can morph into something that will be where her daughter is

Mothers trusted their country
Their men
Their school

With their daughters
Their continuance of themselves
Their secret best friends

Only to be returned ghosts and blank stares
It's sad
I am broken for them

Women worn old rubber band thin with worry
I am sad
But even more so
I'm embarrassed

The best I can do is send a token of condolence
When they've spent more days awake hoping
They could see a face that could only surface with a force
of faith, and that haunts me

I really don't even wanna say "me" in this situation
I just want to speak to- speak for them
Show them that their hoping is not in vain

I remember
They still have not brought our girls back
And no gala, fancy song or hashtag has changed that

So maybe I'll just pray

THE FUTURE

Young black king
Young black queen
Royalty handpicked as the best to represent
So that people with white yellow and red skin
Don't see our high yella mocha brown or black skin and
say, "What up my nig"
In an effort to make me feel comfortable

I wanna be able to travel the whole globe
And not once be mistaken for a hip-hop rapper
I want you to make us all look like a bunch of
accomplished benefactors

You wear the crown given to you by the people
You are now more than just an equal
You the future; are the very thing we the people strive to
equate to

People can't mistake the regal when they see you
Dressed up or broken you're still beautiful
Hey young black king
Hey young black queen
Look well after your kingdom
And the world
Will follow suit

LIFE

This is the longest part of the book, and for good reason. People have always told me that I have lived many lives, or my life should be turned into a movie. Folks get so into it when I'm telling stories, it's as if I'm a sailor or warrior back from a long journey far away. I don't know, maybe it's the Sagittarius in me. Big Jupiter energy. I'm pretty good at story telling. In my life I have lived as open as possible, embracing every experience that comes my way; for better or worse. The following pages contain the experiences I've had breathing. A take on my human experience thus far.

ROOTS

People often question what I was raised as
Christian or Atheist?
Republican or Democrat?
Black or African American?
Boy or Girl?
My mother raised me to be happy
Showed me that saying hello don't hurt a thing
And smiling is just exercise
Armed me with facts like a hug can save the day
Never hold back joy

THE JAR

Once I knew a beautiful brown girl, a beautiful brown girl with bright bows in her hair that

Skipped
       Through
              The
                      Air

Like meteors in the night sky
She always kept a smile, a gift of kindness for everyone in her aura, and a backpack filled with paper, pencils, and pens for class, and a jar full to bursting with small rips of paper She would keep this jar under her desk, ripping off small corners of her test and shoving them in her jar Her eyes bright and glowing like she was handing a new baby to its mother she cherished these strips of paper as if they were what was keeping her alive At the end of class, she would tuck her jar in her backpack and head home

This young girl performed this ritual day after day, until one day, I was walking around the corner going to get a burger and I saw her crying on a curb, huddled over her jar, her tears smearing the ink on the small ripped pieces of paper. Heartbroken I sat beside her, but before I could speak, without even looking at me, her freshly tear stained eyes locked on her jar intently she says, "It's ok I'm just counting See whenever God gives me tears, I count them while I count my blessings My tears always lose to my blessings." Astounded I sat next to her as she read her blessings. Smiling and glowing a little more with every layer of the jar gone. Soon, she was brand new
That beautiful brown girl; a beautiful brown girl with bright bows in her hair that

Skipped
    Through
        The
            Air

Like meteors in the night sky
Whoever thought the cure to misery could be a good memory? I applaud her being She made me see the blessing in living, in forgiving Forever changed I walked away, because if she could keep her head up then I could too She blessed me with the gift of sharing this story with you

SONGS

I love the songs the songs that get me in the mood, the songs the songs that make my body move, the songs the songs that, started revolution

And I bet you they had a theme song for the constitution, and I've concluded that even know the reason why remains elusive everything can be changed by music

Marvin was right when he sang, *"music is my heart and soul"* Because it's been told that music can make a weak man grow bold, leave a crying baby consoled, make a love affair unfold, shiiit I bet music inspired your next poem

So, who's to say these drum beats and melodies don't contain potency after it had my people, Wading in the Water, during slavery, We Shall Overcome made it unacceptable to be separate but equal and we all know Bob Marley made songs for the people

I love the songs by Hispanics, whites, blacks, Asians, Jamaicans, Australians all around to every nation Yes, I love music by every kind of thing you could think and it's because music is about being, there's nothing more freeing than a song that can direct your thinking sinking into your subliminal easing its way into your dreaming

I love the songs that carry intricate simplicity, because music marks the times like the archives of history Whoever thought we could accomplish so much by just listening?

I look at music the way I look at poetry, as if it's what's molding me
It was the music of the Israelites that made the walls of Jericho fall, music that made young soldiers fight with their all, music will have you rethinking life like, What's Going On?"

My songs are the only reason I don't lose it
It helps me live what I say I didn't have to write this to
prove it, but I did so you'll feel me when I badly singing,
"OH! Just like music!"

THOUGHTS OF MAYA

There's a funny thing about sunshine
It's as infectious as past times

All we want is peace
Or even a little piece of mind
A place to find the meaning of our existence

We play victim and survivor but only on dry land
Only the brave are deep sea divers

The few inspire the dreams of the many
The many exploit the dreams of the few

But we still
Wait for sunrise
Frolic in the sunshine
In the night
We compromise
Because sometimes
Every once in a while
There's no difference between day and night

EAR TO THE STREETS

I'm trying to use my creativity to say something that's gonna make y'all FEEL ME

Say something to move you and sprinkle that special, sparkling, tingly, like the poetry your ears are worthy to hear

I don't want to half step on this
There's been too many times, while caught up in my own personal time, I've used my poetry to give you an explanation of me, instead of something to feed you mentally

I yearn for inspiration that would make my words so deep that they appeal to your aesthetic
Like my words will compare to the purple haze cast by Jimi
I want you to hallucinate while I'm speaking

Sit back and see how far the rabbit hole goes
I wanna pique your curiosity like sex to a young woman in chastity, keep Pushing until you feel a break in your pubic
Let me mind love you like you've never been loved before

I wanna say something to make you FEEL!!
I guess the best thing for me to do, is
give my ears to you

Make my words influential like Facebook ads, I'm in your mental
I wanna put my ear to the streets literally, I wanna document every pebble
I wanna count the woes of every teen age pimple tell of things complex and simple
From the problems with geriatrics, to hurt little girls, to crooked police tactics

I want to be T.I always know "what's up and what happening" Comment on how people are acting, remind folks that the pain is just fraction
This a big life we lead

Short
Precious
Blank
And pure

All we need do is add the happy little trees, and the playful fluffy clouds and the sturdy little bushes
Make a portrait the world will remember
I wanna be a storyteller
Keep my ear to the pavement
Document how humanity made it

That way I will always
Have something
To say

ODE TO PLAY, PLAY POETS

I spit this poetry to battle all the folks spitting with halitosis. You know, the folks that seem to induce a hypnosis that causes the broken to fall to the wilds of the richest interests cause that's what makes America glisten. Look at that sweet sweat roll down the backs of black, brown, and latinx slaves I mean, the NFL, the NBA. Put your feet in their shoes and walk the paths made from the tears of natives. Continue to be unaware that we, the conquered, succumb to this blatant bloody cadence. Following a binary moral code of right and wrong. Hegemony set in motion by a white man's constitution we all patronize and abide by. What do you stand for? They say stand for something, or you'll fall for anything, but stand for everything and you'll never have a day of peace. We all have a choice in the way we use our voice, so tell me poet.

Do you care to truly study the semantics of your ideals, or are you blinded by your zeal?

LONELY

The drugs are gone
I'm all alone
My face is over on my bed side table
My smile and personality
Are being cleaned in a jar on my bathroom sink
It's just me
The drugs are gone
I'm lying in bed with slow music on
Thinking of you
Wondering if you approve of the dirt I do
Thinking of my empathy or lack there of
Breaking one heart after another
Always a different muse
I'm not scared of shit
But myself
The drugs are gone
It's 3 in the morning
I can't close my eyes
Pictures of people dying, crying, and screaming
Keep floating through my mind
My nightmares
Are gonna suck tonight
Seeing death just ain't natural
Wake up screaming with your sweat cold
The drugs are gone
I'm all alone
I'm lost
Ready to take the journey home

NOTE ON LIFE #1

August 8, 2018

They never tell you how MESSY healing is. I remember my mother used to fall on her knees at the church alter some Sundays and just cry. I mean CRY. I never understood. I would just hold her hand. I get it now. She was healing... I am overwhelmed at this point in my journey with all the things I'm allowing myself to finally feel. (Without freaking out or shutting down) I'm working through the muck of 20 years of pent up emotions. Being WHO I AM and all that encompasses unapologetically. Learning I am not on this realm to please you. I have seeds to plant, a legacy to build. I am bursting and ready but still a little scared to embrace me and let loose of the world. Trying to change the last of these bad habits. Holding my hands back from beating on myself. Learning that tough love ain't the only love. Growing, experiencing, changing. #notesonliving

NOVOCAIN

We find it hard to feel
Hard to just stretch out our arms and just
Cry
Cry like it really does release endorphins
Cry like we want a good night's sleep
Cry like a child
'Cause it seems like only children are willing to cry
Be tickled
Like only the young can enjoy unbridled emotion
When you grow up it's time to cope
SHOOT
SMOKE
TOKE
Take away tears, Falsify smiles
Because scarred tissue, has no nerves
And we're all healing from something

LIFETIMES: A SHORT STORY

I used to visit an old woman. Though her home was dirty and tattered, bug infested, and foul smelling; what made me keep coming back was the pictures on the wall. They were all pictures of this model, a gorgeous exotic woman with smooth tan skin, dark long brown hair, legs to die for, and blazing auburn and blue eyes that made you want to cry from joy just looking at her. She travelled the world in those pictures. I wanted, I needed to see them. So, every day I would go, and knock. And wait for the gnarled toothless, eighty something little dirty smelly grey eyed woman to creep to the front door and let me in to her little home to sit on the dusty floor. (She sold the furniture a while back, I hadn't bothered to ask why.) I would gawk at the pictures on her wall while she while she rocked and swayed standing at the window; unaware that I was admiring the woman on her walls. One day, while laying on my side, looking at my favorite picture of the model speed boating in Spain that hung over the mantel piece, I asked the old lady, "Why do you keep these pictures of this beautiful woman? Is she your daughter? Do you know her?" She finally looked from the window for the first time and gazed at me. Her glazed pale grey eyes filled with tears as she smiled and said, "I keep them because I need to remember. No, my lovely, she is not my daughter and no I don't think I know her much anymore..." I ruffled my face, "Anymore? So, you did know her once!?" My eyes caught fire with excitement. I needed to know who this woman was! She replied in a descending tone, "I was her... once..." as she turned back to the window. She rocked and swayed. In that moment, a pit caved its way into my stomach. I finally looked around the pictures. I finally allowed myself to see the crack stems and syringes that littered the floor. The burned spoons and empty baggies. Newspaper clippings from car crash and obituaries of a man and two beautiful children. Ripped tear stained holiday cards littered the floor. And she swayed and rocked… as I quietly clicked the door closed.

STUPID QUESTIONS

Once I asked a man that couldn't use his legs
"Why are your shoes worn?"
To which he replied simply,
"Because I try to walk every day."

ODE TO THE LORDS OF THE STREET: A CREATION STORY

It was dark in that section 8 apartment. So, he said, "Let there be light." Got him 28 grams that took him 6 days to flip and on the 7th day, he rested. Probably why he thinks the hustle makes him God. He believed in himself more than he believed in monsters. The monsters were normal people. They walked and talked like they were his equal. He seen crack fiends sell dead babies for narcotic induced dreams. Made a career of selling death as way to depreciate the grim reaper. He hated that black cloak and hood that stalked his hood, made him seem like a limiting factor. Long as there was a demand for them grams, he would be the benefactor. This god had pipe schemes; he made it off broken dreams. When they questioned him, he took the Nino Brown defense. You know, he was just a product of his environment. In the beginning it was all fun as games. He loved the compliments, being flashy. People respected the money in his pockets, not how he got it. Yet even after all the love he was still lonely, so he found him a lump of pink clay and created a man in his own image. Fancied himself a Lord, but he forgot the responsibility that comes with creating things he only thought to be figment. His motions became malignant. The man he created began to regulate his decisions. Maybe it wasn't best to lead his creation to become a victim of the system. He took a step back, appalled at the world he made. He figured the only way to save what he created would be to die in its place. So, he martyred himself so that what he molded would not end up desolate. He was a savior to the cycle he started. All he wanted was to see his way out of the darkness. Ended up with millions of minions enslaved to what he created being thoughtless.

NOTE ON LIFE #2

June 26, 2019

While on this journey of becoming more self-aware I have learned something about myself. I have the gift of vision and manifestation. Not being aware of it so long has produced some disastrous results. For real y'all. I can laugh about it now, but it was bad. But trauma has its perks. People say I'm spoiled. I used to just be like, "I get what I want." *Shrug* Nope! Turns out, I just have the gift of sight. When I see what I want, I make it happen. Ok. Now what??? *Whispers* (There is purpose in you.) I am finding that there is gratefulness and mercy to be found in our gifts. I am grateful to God, my ancestors and angels for their mercy, patience, and grace. For protecting me and my gifts through this journey. I'm also finding responsibility. We have to learn to be responsible with our gifts. Learn to feed them love and hone them to be the most beautiful parts of us. I want to make the ones watching over me proud. Learning to use the tools I've been given. #notesonselfawareness #notesonliving

THAT ONE TIME I WAS GONNA RAP

Take a Kit Kat break nigga/ you ain't ready for war/ I'm getting grimy on niggas turning their girls into whores/ I cop that Columbian bang bang/ straight from the shores/ you figure you the champ?/ I'm about to close that door/ fuck opening a window/ I can stop your wind flow/ turn you from a gangsta to a Winslow/ the first time you hear the chop blow/ more crooked than Gestapo/ show your mama real sorrow/ keep fucking with me/ your next 48 is on A&E/ we all like to watch dead men walking/ my niggas don't possess MOrals but they pump MO rounds/ make you niggas redefine daps and pounds when my niggas start going off Rambo style/ I look on like the ringmaster cause it's a circus when my crew go wild/ Fuck with me/ I'm fucking with your wifey and your first born child/real niggas give a fuck about who dying/ you know good and damn well that I ain't the one for trying/ try and talk shit/ get put down like a bad pit/ any nigga think they legit can get their wig split/ I'm sick like big bear vomit in a poop pit/ still holy like my house is the pulpit/ you got a clean bill of health/ count on your wealth to get you a team/ I like that/ you'll be surprised when you feel that shell/ your body slipping to hell/ I'm crack hard/ fuck with me you won't be doing too well/ keep it pretty and cute my dude/ we got drugs to sell/ anywhere that Mike Mic bang you know my name ring bells/ go head and ask about me/ the hood will tell you the real

ME AND MY MANS JAY

Me and my man's Jay got to smoking some blunts one day and he say,

"Mike, I wish I could get a big ol' gun and strap it to me like they do in Africa cause it's a jungle out here"

I thought to myself, HELLLL YEAH
Addicts haunt the backgrounds of tourist pictures
America has fallen victim to exploiting innocent, inciting ignorance
It's like a game the world plays these days
Nobody has the real story
Everyone's fighting for two seconds of glory Sometimes, for the cause it gets gory
Corporations claiming to fight for change but really
They chasing clout living off bitterness and rage
What happened to the unsung heroes?
Once we were coming to realize dreams of equity
Then the white house coined tel pro'd like a pro
Now America is in a cold race war
Your outward appearance determines your character
I'm really thinking equality is unattainable
But then my man Jay say

"The bullshit can't reach you if you're unavailable it's crazy out here, got to keep our blinders on like horses at the fair it's a shaky ground we stand upon
best believe we gon be prepared"

B-L-A-C-K

Give me my B-L-A-C-K
Gimmie that middle passage great minds that never landed
Gimmie that roots that, officer overseer
Gimmie that Underground Railroad
Harriet Tubman
Give me upset families with no husbands
Civil war
Give me the victory and not a lick more
Give me the Deep South and the original Jim Crow laws
Gimmie the Mississippi church burning
Give me four daddies with no daughters
Chase me with angry dogs and spray me with high pressured water
Segregation riots
GIVE ME MY B-L-A-C-K
Gimmie black progression
Now we pilots, Tuskegee airmen
Gimmie that Malcom X
That Thurgood Marshall
W.E.B Dubious
PLEASE
Give me a voice!!
Then give me violence
Gimmie Rodney King
Gimmie OJ Simpson and put Johnny Cochran on the scene
Gimmie hate crimes
Give me all the slain black faces on a slate and a good look at the times
There's no better time than the month
Or
Make it the year
Every day is all about B-L-A-C-K
I know my black ancestors got my back
So give me my B-L-A-C-K
And let me follow their lead

Cause this blood in my veins untamed by the multitudes
of my ancestors slain
Don't run thin
It runs
B
L
A
C
K

NOTE ON LIFE #3

March 24, 2018

Let me tell you something about trusting in something higher than yourself. Anyone that has ever did me wrong has never succeeded in a real way. I've been watching. I've been waiting. Things fall through, folks stay in the same place, things never really fall in line for them, it's always a hustle etc. As LONG as you are hurting people, or not treating people with love and compassion you are blocking your blessings. I see a lot of people that ACT nice and loving, but they are not. People see that. They treat you as amazingly as you treat others. Life is about the impact you make, not the cool stuff you can do. I speak the truth about people, but I love them regardless. Sometimes despite themselves, sometimes from a distance, but I'm always right here. Even for people I don't care for. God didn't put me here to pick and choose who and how to love. He put me here to show that love is. Some people take this world by storm because they got heart... you got to trust that whatever whomever got it beating in the first place, loved you enough to set all this in motion. Treat the world how love has treated you. No matter what the world does. Promise you'll be great.
#notesonliving

BLACK GIRL MAGIC

Black boy asks, "Are black girls really magic?"
Black man answers:
Black girl fell from tree once, a tree called grace
Black girl got scared
Black girl got tortured
Black girl was molested
Black girl raised foreign families, patched her own
Black girl lost fathers, uncles, brothers, and sons
Black girl wept like the rain season
Black girls been ugly
Black folks were slain
Black girl started #BlackLivesMatter
Black girl was the first to say #AllLivesMatter too
Black girl nursed white and her children
Fed them life
BOY
White and black alike EXIST because of black girl
Yet black girl was rejected by her own kind
Black girl was divided but
Black girl wasn't conquered
The bible says
If man stops his praises the stones will cry out
I guess that's why they say that
BLACK GIRLS ROCK
Black girl still thankful
Black girl still beautiful
Black girl still kicking
Black girl still believing
Black girl still got faith
Even Job and Jesus gave in a little
But not black girl
Black girl took all that
And abracadabra
She turned into black woman

Now you tell me,
What's more magic than that?

HANDS UP

Hands Up!
Hands up I say!
Overseer
Overseer
Officer, Officer
HANDS UP
"Please, I'll do whatever you want"
"Just don't hurt me"
My hands were up
But in defense to my surrender I was punched
And tackled
Put in a choke hold and slammed against computers
I could have been Eric Garner or Michael Brown
FRATERNAL ORDER OF POLICE
Tell me a reason besides my skin color that I am a threat
Why must you protect yourself from the unarmed
YOU
Hold the power
That standard issue 9mm
Has taken away so many standard issue lives
Tell me HOW do you sleep at night?
You arrest journalists and allow hate groups to assemble
My queen got punched in the face by the KKK
And you're worried about brown people in pain?
Again, I say
HOW do you SLEEP?
One day soon the people will rise up
Then what will you do boys and blue
When the guns are taken and turned on you?
Hands Up!
Hands up! I say!
Laws are created with the golden rule in mind
But you undermine justice
Seeking a collar
My heart breaks when I see a strong brown king break
With terror in his eyes, a foot on his neck
And all you can hear is HELP ME!

Or I CAN'T BREATHE
Do they teach you in the academy that life has no meaning?
Do they brainwash you so that you have no gender no ethnicity
Just the blues?
I would like to know what goes through your mind
When you see dead bodies lying on the ground for hours at a time
Do you hurt for the mothers?
Does your honor waiver when you see terror, mistrust, and helplessness in the eyes of those you claim to "protect and serve"?
SPEAK UP!
If you are not the overseer that we see you as then
DO SOMETHING
On behalf of you brethren
FUCK the press
Protect your citizens from each other
Do not protect yourselves from the people
We do not need to be contained or controlled
We need protection from injustice
Hands up
Remember your oath
Hands Up
Remember you're human
Hands Up
Remember your mercy
Hands Up
Remember the slain
Hands Up
On your knees
Assume the position

TROUBLES OF TIME

I shed a tear once for a man who couldn't cry
He said, "I done seen so much pain, I think my tear ducts are dry"

I said damn big man, made me understand you not supposed to cry he said, keep living and you'll learn that's all a lie…

This man was a behemoth, black as night, a sword flaming and bright, with a head filled with worry lines, it was obvious this man had seen the worst of times not the best of times, JUST the worst
So, he took off his dirty hat and with that he began to enlighten me

He said
Chile, I done been HOODWINKED, BAMBOOLZED, CONFUSED, BRAINWASHED
Into believing the lies of the constitution

I've seen blood and war
I was a guard during the Holocaust, and I saw what it cost to believe beyond life
Chills ran up my spine as I saw them willing themselves to die
Protesting, God will understand

I knocked down the Berlin Wall with the Germans
Marched with the Blacks in Revolution
Became a victim of persecution all because I believed in an equitable solution

I saw the bodies that paved back roads in Rwanda
I was a black body calling for help but I was ignored by UNICEF because to them it was just another group of niggas rioting

I tried to believe in unity until life taught me one thing
money changes human beings
I saw cracked out mothers sucking on glass dicks while
people that looked like them were making a profit

I tried to be a NARC so I could stop it, but the
government strung me out undercover and I found that
crack could cure your softness

I learned not to be honest because honesty will not give
you the highest honor in society
Like the politics should be in a democracy
Usually states that WE the common people will inevitably
be overlooked by the 1%

But if you got a gimmick then you cool like ICE
That's why people will vote for a man that grabs vaginas

I walked by the Columbine, Pulse, Sandy Hook, a church
in South Carolina where shots were fired
I was a grown man and I cried
I couldn't be superman and save lives
So I just let their screams fill me
I wish the shooter would have shot me, but instead, I was
just passing by

On the night 9-11 I stood looking at the ruins of building
That day I had been a firefighter on the 10th floor, I
heard the bodies falling from the sky screaming past the
windows

If I could only think fondly of past times
Don't ever wish to live forever, we are already in hell,
released at the very least we can find heaven
I'm an old man that the world has torn to pieces
I guess in one way or another we all end up like Jesus
Bruised and beaten

PANDORA'S BOX

It's dark in here

Nobody wants to be the villain
I guess God named me Nobody and sent me here to reside
I wish I could bring you sunshine and the joys of life
Like an early springtime
However, all that lives in me
Are the reasons behind the worst of times
I was supposed to keep hidden from you
The gods were supposed to allow you to walk in this realm relatively pain free
But
If that's how things are supposed to be
Why do these feelings exist inside of me?
Maybe's it's because the gods made Pandora
Just
Like
You
She was curious about the things that I could do
Unintentionally she released me upon you
I don't mind the haters
I am the very being that drives you to anger
Makes you kill that man
Lie on that stand
Turn your back on your fellow man
It's all because of me
I am the negativity that can never be resisted
Walls have crumbled behind my antics
My heart break has caused kings to become manic
When my heart rate goes up mankind begins to panic
I am tribulations sweet release
You personify me with your every bad deed
Every bad seed sown with the best of intentions
Is reaped by my scythe into a harvest cycle of victims
The black sheep of this world are my minions
I am the Mayweather of devastation

I am the whisper in your ear
That makes it hard to fight temptation
I am the dictator of purgatory
You will never rid yourself of me
Despite all this, folks still lived, took on the risks
When you stood in the wake of your devastation
I saw a chain reaction trend amongst the nations
You began to rebuild
You began to balance me with the good things
I understood that my actions gave you pain
But I also gave you hope
I gave you an excitement for life never felt before
Now you people just couldn't wait to endure
Take me on and give this hell I bring what for
So now I'm happy Pandora opened the door
I'm the feeling that everyone needs
But no one wishes for
I am the things nobody wants to say
The secrets you stuff in the closet and tuck away
Take any road you want, but I am the only way
I am Pandora's Box
The reason you are thankful for this day

NOTE ON LIFE #4

October 21, 2018

Coming out of a depression is like waking up to a gentle breeze with a face full of sunshine the day after a tragedy. It's like being full after fasting for a long time. It's like a glass of water after 3 days of dry heat. You remember the pain. Vividly. But somehow you also feel a distance from it. Like you can't remember what it was like to not be ok, but you can't remember the last time you were really ok. Sometimes I just lay here thinking about all I've been through emotionally over these last couple of years. How I've changed... I still go through ups and downs but knowing yourself is the battle (Not half of the battle, it is the battle) I was incredibly sad for a long time. I can say that now. I understand what has happened in my life, and who I am because of it. Now, I can finally move forward. #roadtoredemption #notesonliving

LETTER FROM A QUEER TO THE WORLD

To whom it may concern,
Most of us
Are ripped battered and torn from dark closeted pasts, we come from childhoods where we were mostly shadows and masks

Queer:
An adjective to describe something strange or odd

When I was young
People would ask me who I wanted to grow up to be
I would always say, normal
I was aware at present I was not
These buds of self-doubt grew
Bloomed and showered my senses
Shortly after I reaped my first harvest of self-loathing
People always ask me what "queer love" looks like
And I tell them, it looks like rain in a dessert
Like snow in Johannesburg
Like a dirt road through a thick forest
Like lighting with no thunder
It looks like love where you didn't think it could be
It looks as hard fought for as it feels
It looks like weeklong romances ending in marriage
Maybe we do get married too quick
But it's only because our longing to build something beautiful from the ruins of such early trauma and heartbreak is overwhelming
We've been fighting to be seen since before we could remember
To be understood
So, we hug strangers
Hold parties for people that act like us
Create spaces void of family and maybe some friends Call it safe
Constantly searching for comfort from our demons
We reclaimed the word love from churches

Like black people did nigga
Threw some glitter on that bitch
Re-branded it as a verb
We did what they thought we couldn't
We survived
Together

LETTER TO THE BIGOT

A letter to the man who believes God has made mistake in creating me

God has no gender, but is three beings
We are all trying to be more God-like

God gave me a quandary and helped me through strength to show who I can be despite my circumstances

God gave me testimony
My heart and life's purpose are all for the glory of my maker

God's goal is to create life that will praise the creator

No.

Mistake.

Here.

NOTE ON LIFE #5

June 12, 2019

Hey y'all. Still here. Working. Loving. Connecting. Growing. I remember I just wanted to be normal. Until I realized, normal is just what regular is for you. It's what you chose to make your everyday. This lady told me, "you need to keep your support system elevated." Basically, if you have some sense, keep people around you with some sense. Doing the work to become aligned has shown me a lot of nasty things about myself. It spurred me even more to be "better" made the perfectionist in me produce so much angst it began to turn into self-loathing. (WHAT IS WRONG WITH ME??) I had to understand that we all have a dark side... In accepting that I find I need to learn to be more compassionate with myself and others. This journey is a journey. It takes time. I feel myself changing. Trying to bloom through what seems like concrete sometimes. So now one of my affirmations is, "You are not perfect, you are your own normal." I just always felt like, if I was perfect, if I was normal, if I could just be good, everything would always be ok, people would be nice to me and care about me. That was just me trying to play the game with a controller with no batteries. No one in this realm is in control. I am learning to trust, take risks, not be normal. Just be ready and willing to make the best of this journey. ♥♥♥ #notesonliving

SACRIFICE IS SO SACRILEGE

So, a while ago I was talking to my mom, venting about some bullshit as usual, and she rolled her eyes and sighed. When I asked her what was wrong she simply replied, "Your problem is you don't understand sacrifice." At first, I took her critical assessment of my ranting as an insult. I know about sacrifice. Then I really thought about it and read about it for a couple of months. I read about a woman who had 6 siblings 4 of them younger than her. Her mother and father worked as hard as they could to provide for their family, but they were just barely getting by. The young woman wanted to be a doctor. But instead of going to medical school or even college at 18, she signed up for the military. Signed away her dreams of scholastic achievement. I thought about how maybe the determination for a better life might have outweighed her disappointment. I then thought about my mother who told me when I was in high school, she denied herself lunch and walked to work every day for a month to buy me a laptop that I had been asking for. I read that sacrifice by its third definition means to give up something valued for the sake of something else regarded as more important or worthy. In essence my mother's hunger was nothing compared to my materialistic needs. Think about anytime someone has gone without so that you could have. Think about how many times you've gone without so someone else could have. Honestly think about it. Then, I thought about how the idea of sacrifice effects black people in America as a community. Again, I learned something from my mother. (she's great with this stuff) She had been paying this black man and his son to do her lawn and cut back some trees. While they were working, a rock had flown from under the lawn mower and shattered her back door. The man and his son offered to pay for the damage and finish the lawn at a discount. This whole time these other guys (I won't name their race) kept coming by asking to do the lawn. Their price was lower, and they would have most likely done a quicker and better job. When I brought this up to my mom she just shrugged and said, "I rather uplift and invest my own people than another's simply out of convenience. If we don't even give our own a chance how can we expect people that don't look like us to?" From this I learned that we as a community don't sacrifice much at all. We don't boycott rappers who have stock in jails and whose interests are in sending as many people there possible. The beat's cool and we just got to be cool. So, we'll say whatever, "kill that nigga, I suck dick, rob that bitch for looking at me funny, fuck bitches get money." We don't do things to prove we are not what anyone looking at us says we are because people pay too much to keep us silent. We don't stand up and say I don't care if I don't eat, if I can't find a good job, if my kids don't have the best life, you can't buy my dignity.

We are missing sacrifice. So, we get to dancing. I read the MLK bio a while back and was surprised to learn his family wasn't all the way gun ho about his activism in the civil rights movement. It scared them. He sacrificed his own safety, his family's happiness and safety because he believed that we as a people could be better. After studying sacrifice, I have been tremendously humbled. I have realized the ways I have been part of the problem. I just wonder if I will be able to carry out my deed of sacrifice when the time comes.

NOTES ON LIFE #6

November 5, 2018

BELIEVE people when they show their true colors. I am worthy. I am amazing. I work hard. I give love. And now I understand... hurt people need a little more help. Hurt people. Hurt people. So I love. Despite people's reaction to it #**loveanyway** Don't be scared to protect yourself. Defend yourself with love of self. It doesn't matter how they hurt you, you have you. You're wonderful and beautiful. We all are. In our own way. Karma is real. God is real... Have faith. Love on in a world that, at first, discouraged your smile.

I put this in the book at first and took it out because I was afraid of losing the person referenced here. Since talking to my friends about rejection and reconciliation I decided to put it back in. Someone may need to see this. The text is the last text I sent to a woman I was dating for a while off and on. She replied back to "I love you." by rolling her eyes. I can't do anything but laugh about it now. I get it. Shorty's life is miserable, all she does is cry. I can't expect her to have love for me when she ain't even got it for herself. However, I still got love in my heart. She could never dilute my joy with her misery, but she damn sure tried. Women come and go out my life, all of them with lessons and blessings to share. Some lessons are harder than others. This one was a hard one. Y'all the heart is a muscle. I'm learning that sometimes, you got to work that bitch so hard you can't move it the next morning, but it's just gonna make you grow. Be determined to be the BEST person you can be. Because this world will hurt people until they are a shell of themselves. Be a shelter in the storm not part of the storm. Fight the power, love on. #notesonliving #lovehurts #lovealwayswins

NOTE ON LIFE #7

Aug 16, 2019

When I started returned to therapy, on the very first day my therapist said, "100% of your issues with other people are issues with yourself." At first, I didn't understand. I tried to put it in literal terms,
"If someone hits you with their car in a road rage fight, then that act of aggression is inherently their fault; ergo, their problem has now become my problem because now I'm hit by a car."
She smirked and responded, "NO, now your issue is with your body. YOU chose how you respond to someone else's actions." Biggest thing I had to learn was how to just RELAX. Nine times out of ten folks aren't out here just trying to hurt you. They're not even thinking about you half the time. I had to learn how to let things be, how to let people be. No one owes me anything. I stay out the way, speak when spoken to and help out where I can, love folks when I can, while I can. Conversely, some folks are just shit man. There's literally nothing you can do about that but understand their behavior is due to their own trauma and triumphs. Accept people for who they are, where they are even if it's not with you. It's not about you. How people act is on them. You can't take things personally.

In learning to open my heart I am learning to enjoy my still moments. Not to overthink or dwell on anything but the situations I have control of. People are going to be who they are. That's on them fam.
#notesonliving #roadtoredemption

LOVE

Love is such a powerful force in my life. It has shaped who I am today. There are many forms of love: unconditional love, romantic love, affectionate love, self-love, familiar love, enduring love, playful love, obsessive love etc. I have experienced (and have written about) them all in this part, I think. (Sorry Mom for the expletives!) Love ALWAYS wins; the more I have the privilege of living, the more I am seeing and learning that. I also have learned that love is a doubled edged sword. With its pleasures, it comes weight and responsibility. This part is also about that. It's about me finding my heart in the process of finding some peace, finding confidence, courage, strength, patience, healing, wisdom, focus, discipline; these are all things we need to build a solid foundation of love up under us. Love is the catalyst of all things. Passion. Desire. Fervor. It is what galvanizes us to not only exist, but to LIVE, experience new things, cherish moments. This part is all about the journey that I walk to hold hands in love with not only myself, but with others, and maybe with that special one someday.

LOVE THEORY

When one engages in an act where they are truly connected to someone else; physically, emotionally, spiritually, you start to want to want to become as much of their daily routine as a morning pee

I breathe in

You breathe out

I stretch

You yawn

I smile

You laugh

I get cut

You bleed

I grimace

You shed tears

The sharpest of double edge swords

We

Complete

Us

For better or worse

Zealous selflessness in a selfish world

REAL LOVE: THE DEFINITION

Since my mouth is allergic to bullshit, I guess you can call this the realness

Love exists because we are conscious

We are aware of our inequities

Therefore, we seek acceptance for them in the form of passion

Many people confuse the basics

Wanting to fit love into a persona that is in our favor

However, the danger is that love is not like picking your favorite flavor

After all we never even see the moments we savor

We all close our eyes when it feels good

We are driven by a need to succeed at being sociable

What would this world be without love?

Ideas of love, molded by mothers, furthered by fathers, and nurtured by family to lay the foundation so that I might have my own one day

As I grow, I must find my own personified definition of love

This is the notion that leads me to you

Our conversations console my fears of being inadequate

Brand new attachments come into existence every time we do our business

Thoughts of you are relentless

A mother's love is no longer requested

Now I seek acceptance in your arms

The feeling grows separate from your charms

I begin to adore you for your essence

In other words, I love the fact that you're living

I love you and I would like to ask you to be dubbed my witness

Love is pure and anything that might make you unsure is there to taint it

Love is as blatant as sunshine

This power we share over one another

Subsequently comes with responsibility

Our love is not to be perverted by life's inequities

That's why when my lips part and I start to label you the one

I don't consider it in good fun

Just as love gives us life, love gives us death

That's why it's till death do us part

Now I can't exist without my counterpart

Love is a cycle

There is no hiding from it, and no one will ever be exempt

Affection is a conflation of hearts

But Love?

Love is what sets us apart

UNIVERSAL LANGUAGE

She never wanted to be touched

But she wanted to be human

So she forced herself to be connected

Lured into being molested in vacant bathroom stalls

I believe that's where she lost it

Struck dumb by blows of everything she ever called love; she went numb

Fear was not an option, so she figured she'd give in to the toxins

It didn't feel good but at least it was normal

Grabbed up for kisses

Never good enough to be a wife so she spent her life as a mistress

She found fame in what she never wanted to claim, and they used her

They used her up like the pot she smoked and in return she took them higher

But she got ridged when they tried to hold her

Kept the sheets tight when she slept, she was socially inept

The people that thought that she was cold must have been missing the concept

See she forced herself to be human

Cause she went down for love and came up a victim

Whoever thought this simple feeling could be so addicting

Every night she speaks love like a universal language

I asked her what love was like she like she say,

"You know the late-night love the way you feel when you get a free bag of that good bud see baby, this is the life I just want everyone to remember me"

Shit, I guess you could say she was addicted to making history

MAKING IT THROUGH 2:36 AM

Nonchalant breezes bully the hairs on my neck
Tonight,
Dreams have no meaning,
The moon eases
I recall those giggles in the dark
Appealing
Love mixing with my feelings
Intriguing
Daylight becomes the enemy
Thieving
We live for the night
My heart, gives understanding
To your breathing

BOOGIE MAN

Tune of Mos Def "The Boogieman Song":
*I am/ the most beautiful boogie man/ the most
beautiful boogie man/ let me/ be your favorite nightmare
Close your eyes and I'll be right there *

Maybe I'll call it an expose
Concerning the topic of optics
Like an optical illusion
Every time I speak, I seem to cause confusion
Maybe why her heart has suffered such contusions

I should start from the beginning
On my birthday
I was new but I heard the doctor say
This pretty brown baby is gonna break some hearts
You can expect a lot of pain from a pretty brown baby like this

I frowned in my infancy
It turned into delinquency
By middle school I held no regard for decency
Felt like no one was really a friend to me
Cried frequently

When I was beginning to hit high school
I conversed with a girl I figured was beautiful
Being with her made me feel less alone
Told me she was in a giving mood
Asked me if I'd love her
All I could think to say was yes
I mean
Until I find another
She took it for what it was
That's all I remember of her

Her heart was probably a little tender after
But it let me know that I had a new skill to master

I had gotten a taste of being a heartbreaker

I started to learn the art of flattery
Learned that details don't matter really
Most people will love anything that seems friendly and looks pretty
Can talk nice
Smart as to make you think twice

I know it's not right
I guess I needed the proof
I am really worth loving
If only for a short while
It helps me sleep at night

People always fail to see the dark side
They stare into big pretty tempting eyes
Too mesmerized to see what lies behind
They entrust their trust
Lose sense of what's improper or just
Indifference turns into a must
Craving for just one more touch

Strong feelings of lust that your heart just can't help
All because you took that first step
You closed your eyes and fell asleep
Gave this boogie man in me ample time to creep

I had you freaking
Crying for me because to you I was perfect, dreamy
Then the nightmare leaked in like I was Freddy
I couldn't help myself
Your heart was screaming come get me
I wouldn't have done it if you hadn't made it so tempting

Wasn't I good for you
I good luck green shroomed 1 up'd you
Brought my storm on made you strong

All I know is how to make things wrong
You can't say that you couldn't move on
You were naive and I gave you something to be afraid of

In the closet I sneak
Capturing hearts
Havoc I reek
But then
No one's ever made you see you beautifully
Just like what you do for me
I am the same to you as you are to me
Only until another heart needs this type of saving
Indeed I am not a normal man

*I am the most beautiful boogie man/ the most beautiful boogie man/ the most beautiful boogie man *

GETTING LATE

** It's getting late… Why you got to be here?? Beside me… watching…. needing… wanting…. me…**

Don't need me
See baby it's getting late and the last time I held out my hands to you I pulled back a handful of hate
So maybe it's best if you not spend the night

I don't want things to end up in a fight
Every time we talk about making it right, we go left
Maybe we should just forget

The sun looks the same at dusk as it does at dawn
Either way it's getting late
You shouldn't be here when the sun is gone

I've already daydreamed of what it could be if we decided mutually that we could get it together
But your name brings heart pain
I'm not sure I wanna feel all of that again

You brought the rain and I stood through it
But now I've caught cold and I'm sick of love
You have denigrated my heart by over dramatizing your part now I am in a state of unconditional nonchalance

You taught me love is no art
It's meaningless as a doodle in a college class
Maybe we just took it too fast
Maybe I'm love blinded
That's why I always crash
We should just let this thing disintegrate
I can't trust no woman now
My mind just stays full like a fat man's dinner plate

I think you should leave love
Nothing more we can do
Your leaving time is overdue
It's getting late but I can't fake
Once you're gone, I'll just miss you again
Be ready to make the same old mistakes again

DAYDREAMS IN ANAPHORA

I like that there's holes and ink all over her body, and she reads books while I study them one by one

I like that she's so interesting even when she doesn't open her mouth and most times, she doesn't even want to

I like that she never acts like the fact I can't take my eyes off her is odd, she's all the above, why not feast my eyes

I like that she is never quite what that pretty face and perfect smile portrays, there's always more to it

I like that she's like a journey, like my favorite books, like roman poetry she's like all my favorite everything trapped in one thing

I like that at first, I thought we would connect like me and my mama, but it's much deeper and more astounding than that

I like thinking about her to the point my heart pounds in my chest and I get light in the head, I don't know why she affects me like drugs physically

I like that everything about her is soft and sweet, like my candy

I like that she's so strong and small like bamboo

I like that she is she and knows that sentiment is hell to get a hold of

I like that I say I love her and feel guilty, I should be finding another word instead of disrespecting my feelings, love has never felt this good

I like it too much

DAY AT THE BEACH

Our affair was like cracks in the walls of sandcastles
It was bound to fracture into small pieces
But baby
Wasn't it beautiful before the tide came in?
We even captured pictures to show our friends
Those late nights molded from weak mortar and salty tears
We crafted magnificence like portraits of Jesus
We recreated our idea of resurrection respecting nothing but the time trickling through the cracks
Baby we were bound to fall
But
Weren't we beautiful??

HOW'S THE WEATHER

Lukewarm
Like
One sock on and one sock off
I understand your decisiveness
About living
I'm splitting
Yet
You only speak of heartbreak

NOTE ON LIFE #8

May 5, 2018

The best thing I ever did in my life was stand up for myself. Not everyone deserves your energy.
Sometimes, people were less than warm to me, deceitful, manipulative, or just down right mean, and I took it. I was still kind and supportive to people that didn't even like me. These days, you'll respect and love me as much as I respect and love myself or you won't be talking to me. I don't even look at folks I don't care for anymore, I don't break my stride to say hello, no I'm not coming out to support, and you better not touch me I can't be accommodating anymore. I just can't. I almost lost my mind; hell, almost lost my life. and some folks gossiped, judged, and cheered. Very few folks cared to help. That's when I learned people would rather see you fall. My energy, my being; they are so precious to me now. I finally feel like I'm special, even if it's just to myself. I won't let anyone take that away. Took too long to find. If I'm loving or supporting you, please believe it's a sign of mutual respect and admiration. I'm not mean, just serious about protecting myself. That's the power of self-love.
#notesonliving

PRETTY LITTLE THINGS

Oh all these pretty little things
Oh all these, pretty little things
What am I gon do with these
Pretty little things
What
Am
I Gon
Do with
These
Pretty little things
Do you mind if I feel you
Pretty little thing
Do you mind if I make you my
Pretty little thing
Would you mind if I left you for this
Pretty little thing
Cause all around me it's just these
Pretty little things
I like
Pretty little things

IF I COULD SING

If I could sing
Ohh baby if I could sing

If I could sing I'd sing from the tippy tops of mountain tops let my voice do flip flops as I rock harder than R&B and Hip Hop my song would be never ending like lamb chop

If I could sing, I'd sing a song for you

I'd make it so beautiful that they'd call it art then I'd throw in melodies of Mozart and every note would melt the coldest of hearts like, "let me count the ways" then I'd take you back to the days of Shakespeare when poetry was so beautiful that it made you shed tears

Ohh baby if I could sing

You'd find my harmonies comforting cause every note from my lips would not make you fall but slip into love with me

I'd change your mood with a tune have you wooed as you swoon into my arms and I'd catch you hold you mold you love you gently into the woman that you should be for me honestly, if I could sing, I'd take a page from Marvin's book and tell you my dreams

My songs would outlast time they wouldn't even have to rhyme see you wouldn't mind being blind because you'd find your sight in every half note and every treble cleft of every line

I'd write a ballad so divine I'd sing it while you slumbered I'd be your lullaby your anesthetic to help keep you under I'd have you saying no wonder I love him

'Cause if I could sing

I'd sing for you better than any other make wanna take me home to your mother I'd have you saying no wonder I love him

'Cause if I could sing
Ohh baby if I could sing

** It'd be about you and how I just
Think about
Dream about
Can't be without
You **

At least I'd try to

HOW TO EXPLAIN THE WAY YOU WANT TO BE LOVED TO THE PERSON THAT YOU LOVE

I don't want our love to balance
I want it to be held down
Saturated
Until there is no need for give and take

Like if you conducted an experiment
And you took a flat plated scale
Two cups of sand,
And two stones of the same mold and weight
Then tried to determine which would give you the most stable levelness
My hypothesis, would be the stones

I want us to see eye to eye
I want we to turn anything into one thing
Into us
Into unity

We are not just giving 50/50
We are giving 100/100
I want us to take it all the way
Strong and deep

Like two stones cast in the sea
Of the same mold and the same weight
Forever falling
Everlasting

I KEPT

After we had kissed that first time
I felt like I had finally gotten what was mine

So I kept
Licking my lips
Trying to
Taste your kiss
Trying to
Drink in some remnant of you

Feeling like if I could just sip you slowly
Like Maxwell House you'd be good to the last drop
When I kissed you that first time
I didn't want to stop
I wanted everything in that moment to last forever
For that second, I was on cloud one
There was nothing I wouldn't have done
At that moment when the moon stars and sun moved about our bodies and spun
We had become metaphysical
No longer the mere feeling of lust but it's adoration that makes me stare
I wanted nothing more than to stay right there
From the first time we kissed

I kept
Licking my lips
Trying to
Taste your kiss
Trying to
Drink in some remnant of you

DIRTY, DIRTY LOVE

I wanna be on her so thick
I won't wash away with soap

So tricked out when her friends come over
She'll say our sex life is like the X Games

I wanna be the lump in her throat
Be what gets her goat
Make her crave each stroke
Of my hand on her face
The caress that chills her skin
And makes her goose bumps show

I want her to believe
that it is my respiration
that causes the wind to blow

I wanna be on her mind 'til the point she uses all my catch
phrases in normal vernacular

I wanna drain away her excess like a catheter
Be the "ooo wee" behind her every melody
Cause for a felony
IF not for morality

No, No

I wanna be her justice
The quintessence of her lust fits
I wanna be the best of her bad habits
Reek quiet havoc

I wanna be a beast to say the least
But shit
I still want to be the small things
Like the dust under her feet
On the enamel on her teeth

So, I can shine for her when she smiles
Or maybe
I could be the thoughts that cloud her mind
Or the words she thinks of
When she's speechless
A cause for a new romantic thesis
Or at the very least
An epiphany of new meaning
I want to be on her so thick
I won't wash away with soap
I want her to always
Be covered
In the filth of my feelings

BLESS-ED BE

There's something sacred in the walls of her pussy!

It's like holy water leaking on me

I've sacrificed my pride
Down on my knees
Slipping slits of wet tongue and warm fingers about her altar

God told me not to worship false idols
But I can't keep away from those diamonds at the meetings of her thighs

Soon as she touch me I'm sanctified
And ready to leave her holier than thou
Make her cover me in her protection

Hands grasping my neck as I bury my head in her breasts holding her hips as she takes me in until she feels it in her stomach

She makes one from the two of us
And who can do that but a deity

There's something sacred in the walls of her pussy!

I can't pray without asking for her again
She speaks to me gently as she pleases me
Begs me to empty my life into hers
So that she can nurture it
smitten belittles how she got me

She's perfect
Made in the image of something I've never seen
So how can I not be fooled?

If this was the Dark ages of Europe, she would truly be burned for using witchcraft cause that pussy can make magic happen make men move mountains make empires fall

There is an ancient, bless-ed existence in that pussy
Keep fucking around it'll change the course of your destiny

She'll put it on you and forgetting your power
Because you will become powerless
With one look from those pretty ass eyes
One kiss from them creamy smooth lips
Then she moans and you're ridged in your skin
Ready to walk her hallowed ground from within
I'm telling y'all there are parables in her pussy

Lessons to be learned in the stories she tells through her physical encounters
And I'm devoted to her existence
Not just an addict
An emphatic believer
I need her
Hallelujah
AMEN

THE PROTOTYPE

The way you made me smile was like Disneyworld
Every place you were was the happiest place on earth

The way you'd make me glow was bright as a skyline
As humble as the night light phone charger you had come to love on the side of my bed

You feared the dark
So you light up every room
You lit me up
Ran me amuck
You were crazier than cool
More cunning than the moon
Good God
Y'all should have seen how she made me SMILE
Like I was home

One of two places I could be myself was with her and a mother's arms
Y'all should have seen how she grew me
Made me see the infinite around the rims of my limitations

The way she made me an ultra-light beam
Made me dream
This was different
I was perpetually perfectly smiling
Always
Fucking
Smiling

Life seemed like a cold rain until you were beside me holding the umbrella even though you didn't have to even though you could have been sheltering yourself or anywhere else you were THERE

And because of that I'm ok

You gave me empty cup
Filled it while I drank you
Your affection poured into me was filled with
Blood sweat and patience stained tears
Bae was pure

I wasn't used to this
I meant it when I said I wouldn't do this thing again
I meant it when I said
I wouldn't connect
My cords got crossed and I'm just not wired right

But you seeped into the cracks I have and pulled me together
Now even if you leave
You left me put together

I have no words for how you illuminated me
Like a lighthouse
Like a beacon
Like when you are pulling at straws
Hoping for just anything
Then the BEST THING comes along and takes you home

Like a movie
Like an inspirational talk
Baby you walked the walk and I admire you
It's amazing how you still so damn fine after all you go through I just wanna hold you
Give you the peace you give me

But suddenly we're just friends
And even if this thing is the birthing pains of a new me
Let you be
The prototype

TIMES

When I asked you to leave me alone I meant to say
Leave your childish ways and come grow with me

When I told you to shut the fuck up
I really meant
I want to know that you're listening

Anger, is a protective emotion

When I said you didn't deserve me
I meant to say
WE deserve better than the love we are giving each other

It's funny how things just don't come out right when you're mad
I mean angry
I mean mad
I'm crazy about you

I remember when we thought falling in love would be fun
Like a 90's black sitcom
Now the 21st century has us more worried about retrograde than acting our age

I meant to tell you that none of these fights are worth it
Instead I kept nitpicking
It's funny how we lose sight of what's really important
Trying to fight for what we think is important

When I walked away from you
I meant to stay
I meant to tell you all I love in this world is you
Instead I opted for loneliness

The surety of my shadow comforts me
More than our love ever could

LIVING VS SURVIVING

She says
I live like I've already died before
Like I've been here before
Like passing through is natural

I learn quickly
Forget the things she remembers
I am not an owner of her
More like an extension
I make her feel like life is no big deal
It's JUST Life
Something to do before we die
She said that life scares her
and excites her

I am an adventurer
It is in my nature to roam and wander
Experience all there is to experience in life
She holds the same enthusiasm
In her
I have found freedom to love in a way I never have
before

We wander like magnets
Continually connecting
Love is a pleasant pastime
We enjoy it on our off days
Like Sundays when we have time to drink beer and burn
in the sun
Most days we are building, working together

On our 5th date we spent the day adulting
Something told me we should spend the day learning
We explored how it was to navigate through life

We rode ups and downs like cans on ghetto sidewalks we
learned why we love the people that help us dig a way out
of no way, that day

She says I live like I've already died before
But our life
Makes me feel like I've never lived before
It is the adventure
I've been longing to die for

PLEASE DON'T GO, WE'LL EAT YOU UP WE LOVE YOU SO!

This was the first time I ever met a girl who loved storms

A girl who could hug a hurricane,
A girl who looked for things to go bump in the night
So she could ask them questions about themselves

She is a girl that would've made Dahmer a pot of tea
Ran Bates a warm bath, washed his back
She see monsters as just people
She can sit amongst lions and tigers in the wild
And they will just admire her

She fills beasts with calm and comfort
Making meekness of their roars with her honey dipped voice

She is never afraid
Just poised and accepting

For the first time
I met a girl who is like a red riding hood
A girl who saw the wolf but kept asking questions anyway
My what big eyes you have

She was a beauty that loved beasts
She wanted
To see me roar
Figured this creature she could love though it be rough
She loved the darkness
Embraced it with light and gave it a home
She could match the monster, wrestle a bit
Wake up just as innocent as a babe

She was the soothing Bach that tamed the three headed monster

She is the song
I am changed
Loved
Whole
Purring

Submission comes to only one as regal as she
I seen victims
Got bodies
But her body is immortal
And she begs beatings

She believes them to be the beatings of my heart
How could one start to reject the pious porous preaching she's pied piping into my ear
I must follow

She is Snow White hallowed
Love in the toughest way
Swaying the heart of kings

This was the first time I ever met a girl who loved storms
A girl that could hug a hurricane
A girl who looked for things to go bump in the night
So she could ask them questions about themselves

I hold her hand
And take her
Where the wild things are

WALK WITH ME

This is me stretching my hand out to you
Come walk with me

I can only be what you let me be
I adore your every movement
You are the center of my self-improvement
Come walk with me

Let your hair down and your mind free
I wanna walk hand in hand with you until the end of our time
Let me walk you into a thousand sunsets
Get some water for your mind
In other words
Let me nurture you

To me you're the most beautiful thing since the birth of this earth
All I wanna do is keep you close
Come my love
Come walk with me

You could never be too much
My God given strength is enough
God put me on this earth for you
So there is never one thing you can do
That will make me fall out of love with you

I want you to show you how I can be your angel
Just like the angels are said to be obsessed with human life
I am truly captured by every move you make
God entrusted me with task of making this last
I will not fail in that endeavor
I will always be by your side
I took a lesson from Luminaire
Your every request is my pleasure
The mere feeling of lust could never measure

In my arms is where you will find love takes no effort
Come walk with me

Trust is the only thing I require
When the situation becomes dire you can count on me to douse the fire
Forget the liars that you've met
They were all apart of God's plan
I never wanted to be your friend but
It was necessary I couldn't have you misconstruing my feelings and making me your adversary

I'm almost glad for the heartbreak so that you could see that when it rains it pours
After it showers your pores open and Mama says that's the best time to put on lotion
Let me be your Dove beauty cream

Don't call me Superman, or any other Marvel
I was not sent to gain your admiration
When you smile I feel no gratification
Your very existence is my inspiration
I believe that my only delegation
Is to witness you at your best
I will never say that I was better than the rest
I was just doing my duty

I understand this road will be hard alone Queen
But I'm here for the ups downs and everything in between

So take my hand
Come walk with me

RED BLACK AND GREEN QUEEN

She breathe life in
Until I can't breathe a gasp
She be beauty
And I can't even fathom aesthetics
She be the precipice of triumph
She be worried kings feel like they don't do enough
She want thee to know thy worth
She overstands, overcomes my frustrations
She wears her angst like a cloak of diamonds
She be sunshine
She be bright smiles
She birth burdens for the sake of trial
She brand new moon flowers
I twilight
We dew
Sustainable
She be reason
She be reflection
She be resurrection
She be solace
She be that quiet
I be the Mad Hatter
She be Alice
Do you suppose?
No
She must
Be a wildflower

POETRY COLLECTIONS
published by
CAPTURING FIRE PRESS

The Woman Inside of Me
by Jae Escoto

He Told Me
by Tyler French

Infinity Standing Up
by Drew Pisarra

A Puzzle Is Still Made of Pieces
by Brendan Gillett

Super Stoked:
An Anthology of Queer Poetry from the
Capturing Fire Slam and Summit
edited by
Regie Cabico

All publications are available at Amazon.com

106

www.ingramcontent.com/pod-product-compliance
Lightning Source LLC
Chambersburg PA
CBHW071008160426
43193CB00012B/1965